Ben Milam

Texas Freedom Fighter

Ruth J. Carnes

EAKIN PRESS ⬥ Fort Worth, Texas
www.EakinPress.com

Copyright © 2003
By Ruth J. Carnes
Published By Eakin Press
An Imprint of Wild Horse Media Group
P.O. Box 331779
Fort Worth, Texas 76163
1-817-344-7036
www.EakinPress.com

1 2 3 4 5 6 7 8 9
ISBN-10: 1-68179-070-X
ISBN-13: 978-1-68179-070-1

Library of Congress Cataloging-in-Publication Data
Carnes, Ruth J.
    Ben Milam : Texas freedom fighter / Ruth J. Carnes.–
    p. cm.
    Includes bibliographical references.
    ISBN 1-68179-070-X
    1. Milam, Benjamin Rush, 1788-1835. 2. Soldiers–Texas–
Biography. 3. Adventure and adventures–Texas–Biography. 4. Indian
traders–Texas–Biography. 5. Texas–History–Revolution, 1835-
1836–Biography. 6. Alamo (San Antonio. Tex.)–Siege, 1836. 7.
Kentucky–Biography. I. Title
F390.M67 C37 2000
976.4'04'092 B 21   00026507

Contents

—Courtesy Western History Collections, University of Oklahoma Library

Preface

"Who will go with Old Ben Milam into San Antonio?" the rugged frontiersman shouted.

Some three hundred freedom fighters answered this call to arms in 1835. Colonel Benjamin Rush Milam led his troops into the Alamo City. He fought along with his men and led them to victory against heavy odds.

But that was the last stand for Ben Milam. The brave and fearless adventurer from Kentucky was one of the most daring commanders of his time. He stands tall as a champion of human rights beside Jim Bowie, David Crockett, and William B. Travis. And his famous yell lit a fuse that inspired the settlers to carry on during the dark days of the Texas Revolution.

Chapter 1

Boy of the Backwoods

Somewhere in the rolling hills of Kentucky there lived a boy named Benjamin Rush Milam. He was born on the fall day of October 20, 1788. His father and mother had blazed the trail over the mountains and settled in the wilderness around Frankfort.

Young Ben grew up like a frisky colt running free over the bluegrass meadows. He had a spotted hound. And everywhere Ben went, that dog was sure to go. Sometimes they even ventured into the dark forest, where warring Indians were still holding out in this strange new land. The boy and his dog got into many hair-raising scrapes over the course of his youth.

Yet the place was right for a high-spirited boy like Ben to grow up. He gained independence and a love of freedom long before he became a fearless fighter in Texas.

But life was not all play for the Milam boy. He had to do his share of chores, even if he was the next to youngest child in a big family. All day long he worked and learned how to do things. It was a part of growing up back in those times.

Ben was awakened at the crack of dawn by crowing roosters. The smell of good country ham frying over a flickering fire told him that it was breakfast time. But if all that didn't get the sleepyhead out of bed, his father did.

There was always something waiting for him to do, like thin the corn, stack the wheat, weed the garden, or cut the hemp for rope fibers. Then there was the barn and stable to clean.

When Ben wasn't working with his father on the farm, he was helping out around the log cabin. One duty was to fetch a pail of water from the spring. This was perhaps his favorite job, especially in the summer. Sometimes he would forget about the errand and go off chasing a rabbit, with his spotted dog yapping up a storm.

There was a creek on the way that was fed by water from the spring. Catching crawdads and tadpoles was great, but swimming was better. There was nothing like a cool plunge into the clear, sparkling water. Quick as a flash, Ben's clothes were off and he was diving into his favorite swimming hole.

Time seemed to fly by out there. And when he heard his mother shout *"Benjamin Rush Milam!"* he knew what that meant. He would get his duds on and grab the bucket of water without delay.

Ben learned to shoot as soon as he could shoulder a gun. By the time he was ten, he could shoot an acorn off an oak tree. People hunted mainly for their clothes and food in those days. Since the boy wore buckskins and a coonskin cap, he had to bag a buck or track down a 'coon or two for his new change of clothes.

Wild animals were plentiful. Ben kept a watchful eye out for those that were suitable to eat, such as quail and rabbit. He listened for a turkey gobble or the bark of a squirrel. Then he aimed his gun and hit his target.

He helped to keep the big iron kettle bubbling with tasty stews day after day. There was nothing better than a steaming bowl full of those tasty vittles to fill up a hungry boy. A thick slab of buttered cornpone on the side wasn't bad either.

Ben had no "book learning." There were no nearby schools, so he learned to write and read from his grown-up brothers and sister. They had learned from their parents.

Ben was smart and caught on quickly. He was good in arithmetic. He could figure numbers as well as anyone in the family. When the boy wasn't too tired at night, he studied words by candlelight. Many of these were backwoods sayings that the family had passed down. They were not always spelled right, so his spelling was a sight to see.

He could not read the family Bible or the laws of the land, but he knew what they stood for. His Catholic, law-abiding parents taught their son how to live true and to be a good citizen.

Other homework for youngsters like Ben included learning about trees and plants. People out in the country gathered roots, barks, and herbs to make their medicines. Most of those remedies, to Ben's dismay, were bitter and hard to get down.

These people also relied upon the madstone to heal bites and stings. The flat, porous rock was supposed to draw out poisons in a wound. Whether they learned about this "magic stone" from an Indian medicine man or brought it with them is a mystery. But they believed it was such a super cure that they kept it in a trunk or an old box with their other treasures.

The handsome, dark-haired lad grew up to be a tall young man. When his dark eyes twinkled, the girls were sure to notice. He often went to "frolics." When the fiddler hit his first notes, Ben knew he had to dance. He whirled the girls around and danced to the rhythms of the country music.

He also liked horse races and was always ready to challenge someone. In their races they galloped up and down the hills—not on fancy tracks as they do in today's famous Kentucky Derby.

Every once in a while a fist fight stirred up some frontier excitement. About the worst Ben ever got out of these bouts was a bloody nose or a black eye.

Chapter 2

Daring Adventurer

The United States was a young nation during Ben's youth. The country's first struggle for freedom from England had been fought in 1776. All was well—but the peace and quiet did not last long. England would not give up. The English king sent out his mighty fleet to hijack American ships out at sea.

And still worse, word was out that their army was headed for New Orleans. If England took over that city, they would gain control of the port and the entire Mississippi River Valley.

Thus the War of 1812 was declared against the old enemy—England. The fight was on again for liberty and freedom. There was a sickening dread and fear among the people. Many still remembered the long, hard battles they had fought before.

The call went out for volunteers across the land. When this plea reached Kentucky, Ben Milam knew what he had to do. He must leave the fields and join his friends in the fight. True, he had never been under fire before, but no country could run over his America and get away with it.

Ben remembered the stories about how England kicked up a fuss the first time. He also recalled how they rang the Liberty Bell, and how the patriots read the Declaration of Independence in July of 1776.

The young and fearless Kentuckian unhitched his horse from the plow and picked up his gun. He said his goodbyes. His beloved dog wagged its tail and licked him in a fond farewell. Then Ben joined the army and stepped aboard one of the flatboats headed for New Orleans.

The young soldiers, clad in their buckskins, arrived in the city with the tails of their coonskin caps flapping in the wind. Their guns were loaded, and they were ready for action.

Private Benjamin Rush Milam of the Kentucky Militia was a daring young soldier in the hot and blazing battle. He fought in the wind and the rain and the heavy fog. His regiment was placed in the center line at the main point of attack.

The only protection was a wall of logs chinked with mud. The English soldiers, known as redcoats, kept coming at the young Americans. Bullets whizzed in this fierce fight. But the American rebels turned the redcoats around. They laid down their arms and sailed back to their homeland. The United States of America was free again.

Chapter 3

Adventure on the
High Seas

Ben Milam came out of the shootout safe and sound. He went back to Kentucky and settled down to a peaceful life on the family farm. The family raised big crops, especially wheat. It took a lot of work to get the wheat ready. At harvest time it had to be cut, thrashed, and sacked.

The wheat was made into flour at a mill, which was located on a creek or river. A miller ground the grains between stones that were turned by a wheel, powered by water. Then out came the soft and powdery white flour, ready to use in making good things to eat.

There was more than enough to carry the Milam

family through the year. Since most folks back then grew their own wheat, there was no sale for the extra product. Neither was there anyone around the area to trade or swap with for other things.

The Milams needed money. There was word that the market in New Orleans was good. Since Ben knew his way around the city, he offered to take the surplus wheat down there. He was a little bored with farm life anyhow.

Ben and a friend loaded the heavy barrels of flour onto a barge at the docks. Then they shoved off with the valuable cargo.

They had to watch for signs that marked the dangerous mud reefs and sandbars. Sometimes they had just inches to spare. Once they got through that, it would be fairly safe. However, they still had to keep a sharp-eyed lookout for smugglers and pirates who might be lurking along the shadowy shores.

Ben and his friend managed to cope with the problems, and things were looking good. It seemed as if luck was riding with the happy-go-lucky pair.

Ben felt it wouldn't be long until he was a rich man. He would buy presents for his family and have a good time in New Orleans. Then he would head back with his pockets full of money.

But things had taken a turn for the worse in New Orleans after the War of 1812. The city had been bombarded by a new enemy—an economic crisis. Prices were low and business was bad. Money was hard to come by. Farmers were having to take losses to sell their goods. And the bottom had dropped out of the flour market.

Ben had just made his last round at trying to make a profitable sale. And everywhere he went, he was turned away. He was ready to give it up as a lost cause.

Then he heard about the demand for farm products in Venezuela. Business was booming there. News was they were paying unbelievably high prices for flour. A fellow could get rich in one trip.

It was a long way down to that South American country. Ben had never even heard of Venezuela. And he did not know the first thing about sailing a ship. Also, his load was not that big.

But the spirit of adventure and the chance to make a fortune offered an exciting challenge for him. He reasoned that he had everything to gain and nothing to lose.

Ben, along with some other farmers, chartered a schooner and hired a crew of sailors to man it. They sailed away toward South America.

All went well until everyone aboard ship became ill. Ben thought he was just seasick from the lashing waves. He soon knew that he had something far worse—the dreaded disease called "yellow fever."

He was sick for days. His fever raged, and he had terrible headaches. Ben hurt all over. He was out of his head most of the time. But slowly he began to get better.

In the meantime, the captain and most of the crew had died from the disease. Only a few men were left to navigate the schooner through an oncoming storm.

Waves lashed the ship in fury. Water splashed up over the deck. Sails were ripped away. The ship could sink at any time. All would be lost.

Amazingly, they rode out the storm, and the battered vessel finally drifted toward land. It was a thousand wonders that they ever made it.

Another ship, headed for the northeast coast of the United States, picked up the worn and weary survivors.

Ben Milam took one last look at his barrels of flour before embarking. All the flour was ruined, and so was his dream.

He left the rescue ship at New Orleans, thankful to set foot on solid ground again. Surely there were better days ahead.

Chapter 4

A Long, Dry Trip

Ben Milam's best-laid plans had floated out with the tide. But he hadn't lost his courage. He began looking for work in order to regain his losses.

The depressed young adventurer pounded the cobblestone streets of New Orleans trying to find a job. He knocked on doors but was turned away. It seemed there wasn't anything for him to do. He soon found out that with no education, his chances were slim at ever landing a good-paying job.

But Ben just happened to notice on one of his job-hunting rounds that an Indian was riding up to a trading post. The brave had beautiful horses of different colors and many animal pelts that he wanted to trade for other goods. He was of the Comanche tribe, from the faraway plains of Texas.

A sudden thought flashed through Ben's mind: *Why don't I go to the Indian camps? If I could bring something they wanted, we could swap with each other. There just might be big money in this!*

Ben knew he had a good sense about horses. And he could judge a fine fur pelt when he saw one. Also, he had been swapping ever since he was a young buck—knives, strings, fishhooks, anything. He smiled when he thought of how many times he had bargained with his brothers. And how he sometimes got the best of the deal.

Ben knew that if you can't find a job, well, you make one. He would have to strike out on his own. Since the flour project was such a flop, maybe this one would be successful. He certainly knew more about being a trader than setting out to sea for faraway places like Venezuela.

Ben wasted no time in making friends with one of the merchants. He refused to give up when the man told him that Texas belonged to Mexico, and Spain claimed both of them. Very few Americans in the United States dared to enter that foreign land— mainly murderers who wanted to escape prison, or thieves and pirates like Jean Lafitte and his gang. But, the merchant added, if a man had the grit to go into this wild country and got back safely, chances were he would make a lot of money.

Ben understood the odds, but he felt he had to

go for it. He had to convince the shopkeeper to let him have the trading goods on credit since he had no money to buy such things. He would promise the man that he would be well repaid with horses, pelts, or anything else that might be of value upon his return trip.

Ben sparked the merchant's interest when he reminded him that the incoming farmers would need horses to plow their fields in the Mississippi River Valley. The merchant knew that he must have a good supply to meet this demand.

The trader was smart enough to know that more horses meant more money. He took a long look at the daring young man who was so set on taking such a risk. If anyone could make it, this serious, well-seasoned Kentuckian could. He decided that Ben was someone he could trust. The two men made a deal.

Ben didn't let any grass grow under his feet in getting ready for the big venture. He gathered a supply of bright-colored cloth, ribbons, beads, trinkets, and shiny mirrors for the maidens and the squaws. He picked out pocket knives, tools, and other things that he thought the braves and their chiefs would like to have. And he outfitted a good supply for himself. There was a food bag, a water bag, a bedroll, and guns and ammunition.

He bargained for some pack mules to carry the

load. These animals were as slow as molasses in January, and they were stubborn critters. But he reasoned there was nothing better than a good strong mule on the trail. They were sure-footed and could be kept in line with the lead horse.

Soon Ben saddled up and headed out with his mule team in tow. He had no idea how far Comanche country was, or just what he might be getting himself into.

He had learned a few things from the old-timers who sat around swapping yarns about Texas. First, he must keep riding west. It would take days and days of some mighty hard riding. Finally, he would reach the high plains, where he would spot buffalo grazing on bunch grass. The Indian camps would not be far away on the upper branches of the Colorado River. One thing in Ben's favor was that the Indians of those early times were generally friendly to most everyone, especially a trader.

The first few weeks in Texas were great. The rolling uplands with tall trees and tangled brush brought back many happy memories. Ben was surprised that it was so much like his old home state of Kentucky. When he pitched camp near a clear, winding stream, he listened to the frogs croak and the owls hoot. It was just like being home.

He rode mile after mile through the forest before the tall timbers gradually started to thin out. Spiny prickly pears and mesquite trees full of thorns grew ever thicker. Patches of bunch grass that the old folks had talked about were scattered here and there between the scrubby bushes.

Yapping coyotes and howling wolves added to the weariness of this strange new country. Also, rattlesnakes were on the move, and their dry buzzing sounds could be heard beside the dusty trail. Some even slithered across the path, raising their arrow-shaped heads and flicking forked tongues.

One day a rattlesnake coiled its scaly body right in front of Ben's horse. But just as the poisonous viper was about to strike, Ben jerked the reins of the horse and sidetracked it.

Ben was more cautious where he stepped after that. And he was more careful about where he bedded down for the night. He didn't want one of those critters to get in bed with him. He wished he'd brought a piece of madstone just in case he needed it for a snake bite.

A few nights later he was awakened by something. He sniffed the air. Nothing but a skunk could smell like that. And Ben did not want *that* animal under his covers either.

He just kept very quiet and still. He never moved a muscle. The skunk stomped up and down and all around him. Finally, after what seemed forever, the black and white stinker headed out for new territory. What a smell it left behind! It had definitely sprayed him.

Ben could hardly stand himself for several days after that.

Ben was getting deeper and deeper into the dry Texas plains. He began to wonder if he was lost out in the middle of nowhere. Maybe he was on the wrong trail. Maybe he would never make it. He was very depressed.

Ben couldn't have been any more lonely if he had been stranded on a deserted island. There was absolutely no one to talk to. Earlier he had seen a few Indians and a priest who lived at a mission. But that had been a long time ago.

He kept trudging along, thankful that his animals had fair grazing and water. The sluggish stream he was following provided the water, even though it was a bit stagnant and muddy. This was the Colorado River, which was named by early Spanish explorers when they searched this area for gold. The name meant "Red River," but to Ben it looked more murky than red.

Chapter 5

Trader in Comanche Land

One day Ben spotted something moving in the distance. He stopped. What was kicking up so much dust out there? He rode on a little farther. Then a broad smile spread over his dusty, weather-beaten face. Buffalo!

The happy young man sat tall in the saddle and rode on as fast as his mules could follow. He knew that he would find camp soon.

Finally, he met a brave. They talked in sign language. Then the Indian led Ben to his village, which was located along the banks of the river.

The biggest one of their pointed tepees was where the chief lived. The tribal leader greeted Ben wearing a colorful headdress. Since every feather represented a brave deed, this stern-faced warrior was certainly famous among his people.

A fire smoldered in the center of the room. Members of the tribe were seated on animal skins, which encircled the glowing embers. Many spears and bows were stashed all around. This was where they had a powwow.

Ben showed some of his wares. Then he pointed to the skins they sat upon and to the horses that were hitched out front. The chief got the message.

News traveled fast. Comanches crowded around this strange peddler who had brought mysterious bags of magic. Young maidens squealed with delight. The squaws got excited. And the braves could hardly wait to barter for those wonderful things from the white man's world.

Ben happened to glance up and saw a paleface walking up. *Who in the world is that?* Ben wondered. *Is he a bandit running from the law?*

No, it was David Gouverneur Burnet. He had come to this high, dry country in hopes of curing a lung ailment.

The two young men hit it off from the start. They talked about their bad times, like the disastrous trips each had taken to South America. They both went through some of the same horrifying experiences, though each had gone a different year.

There was also some discussion about the silver

that the Indians used in their decorations. They spoke with the chief about this, but they weren't able to get anything out of him. Ben was still curious as to where they had found the treasured metal. Maybe there was some truth behind the tales handed down from the Spaniards about rich treasures in the New World.

Ben and David spoke of their plans for the future. Each agreed they would like to learn more about this strange land of New Spain. Perhaps it was this venture that caused them to see the great possibilities of the future Lone Star State of Texas.

Finally, it came time for Ben to say goodbye to his friend and to those courageous Comanches. Later he would record in the Milam Papers that "These Indians are the most kind hearted, honest, and honorable people I have ever known."

Ben Milam returned to New Orleans with his valuable load in 1819. He made a lot of money for himself and the kind man who had trusted him. As the crow flies, he had traveled well over a thousand miles.

Chapter 6

Freedom Fighter

Ben Milam's adventure in Texas was such a big success that his merchant friend begged him to go again. But the trip had been too lonely, and it seemed to have lasted forever. The restless young trader was ready for more action in his life.

It so happened that a freedom-fighting general by the name of José Félix Trespalacios had arrived in New Orleans. The battle-scarred veteran was organizing an expedition to free his country (Mexico, which included Texas) from Spain.

The general had sent out a call for volunteers. Word was that he was offering rich rewards for those who joined up for the revolution. This exciting news was spreading quickly throughout town.

Ben Milam decided to pay Trespalacios a visit.

The Mexican officer convinced him it was time to make a final break for freedom. And this time there would be no looking back. They had to fight until the end—win or lose.

Adventurous, freedom-loving Ben liked the general's offers. He would be granted a commission as a colonel in the revolution because of his experiences in the fight against the British in the War of 1812. Besides his army pay, he would receive a lot of choice land and some silver mines.

Since he had been successful in helping rout the British redcoats, he decided he could lend a helping hand to send the royal king's men back to Spain, too. He decided to sign up.

Colonel Benjamin Rush Milam looked handsome in his new uniform. He had dreamed of going places and accomplishing daring deeds when he was running wild in the Kentucky backwoods. But never in his wildest childhood imagination did he see himself doing those things in shapely clothes. Gone were the baggy buckskins and coarse-woven homespuns of yesterday. He tossed his coonskin cap in the air and let out a big yell for freedom.

There were about seventy other fearless men who vowed to fight in this freedom expedition. Some of Colonel Ben's old war buddies signed on. Also coming were Dr. James Long, who now had the title of general, and his men.

Long had been in Texas during a freedom fight that had failed. But he still held a fort at Bolivar Point. He offered the place to train the men in battle maneuvers.

Long said that his fort was just across from Galveston Island, where pirate Jean Lafitte and his gang based their operations. He thought this group would come to their aid since they had helped to rout the British in the War of 1812. And these sea robbers did not like the Spaniards any better than they liked the British. They would rob any ship that waved a Spanish flag. All their valuable loot was stashed away somewhere on the island.

Long's offer sounded like a great idea to Ben Milam. General Trespalacios needed all the support he could get. The dreaded Spanish force had kicked the general out of his own Mexico once before, and Milam was determined to help him even the score.

All agreed, and off they sailed to Bolivar Point on the Texas coast. Revolution was in the air. The shout of "*Viva la independencia*" was heard throughout the ship. This battle cry, which meant "long live independence," had been repeated many times earlier. It was started years before by a Catholic priest who revolted to make his people free. And they were not free yet. This bunch of revolutionaries were determined to make that dream come true.

Mrs. Jane Long, the doctor's wife, made the

newcomers as comfortable as she could. Shelters were hastily built. It would be tough going in such cramped quarters.

General Trespalacios started training the troops. He and General Long did not always see eye to eye. This was just the beginning of many clashes that were to come between the two men. Ben Milam was often the go-between. In his quiet and happy-go-lucky way, he helped to settle many disputes.

There were other problems. Lafitte was in big trouble for his piracy. He wasn't about to take on anything else. So there would be no help from him.

No Spanish soldiers were stationed around the area to fight with, but the new recruits were forced into battle with an enemy they had not expected. Karankawa Indians lived nearby, and they resented strangers invading their territory.

At first the men at the fort sensed a strange smell. It was alligator grease that the natives had smeared over their bodies to keep mosquitoes away. The smell grew stronger as they moved nearer to the fort.

Then came the attack. The tall, tattooed braves shot their arrows fast and furiously. Terror raged.

The bold and hardy soldiers met the challenge just in the nick of time. One Karankawa was raising his long cedar bow and aiming at General Long. And who came to the rescue? Colonel Ben did.

The skirmish was soon over. The cannibal tribe was forced to flee. They rowed away in their dugout canoes, which they had anchored nearby.

General Trespalacios decided it was high time for his men to leave. Luckily, they had driven the natives off, but they had used a lot of the ammunition. They needed to save it for the revolution. A few more encounters like this and there wouldn't be enough left to do any good.

They divided the forces. Long and his men headed for Goliad. Milam sailed with Trespalacios and his group down the Gulf of Mexico toward Veracruz. Both had agreed to meet in Mexico.

The welcome mat was certainly not out for the voyagers in Veracruz. Some of the people and their leaders were Spanish royalists, still loyal to the king of Spain. They arrested Trespalacios and threw him in jail. Milam made such a fuss about his leader being locked up that they put him in jail, too. Ben was sent to a jail further inland.

Little is known about the route this heroic little band took after their release. It is possible that they took the path blazed by the ancient Aztec Indians. They were on the way to Mexico City to join the commander of the armed forces. They trudged mile after mile over mountains and plains, shooting it out with little bands of the king's royal soldiers all along the way.

Ben was wounded badly by a sniper, but the natives in a tiny village saved him. They took him to their hut and helped him get well. They shared their food with him, meager though it was.

These kind people were so poor. They had very little to make their life easy. He noticed they were using a coconut and a raw spindle to make their cloth. It was a slow way to make anything to wear. He wished he could give them a spinning wheel from his country as a gift of appreciation for all they had done for him.

He was alarmed to learn that these people had been at the mercy of Spain for so long. Not only were they not able to make their own laws and hold office—they could not even bear firearms.

Since they could not load, point, or shoot a gun correctly, they were not able to put up much of a fight for the revolution. But they gave their pledge of allegiance to the independence movement. And they had helped by saving a freedom soldier named Ben Milam, who was now well enough to march onward into battle.

It took a while to win the revolution. Colonel Ben Milam stood by his general until the Spanish army waved the white flag of defeat in 1821. But there were still troubles ahead.

A new government was soon set up in Mexico. The country was divided over how to start out because there was so much distrust, especially of foreigners like Ben Milam. He was not a Mexican citizen, which meant to many that he really had no right to say anything. But he felt he had helped win the revolution, and therefore had a right to voice his opinion.

This got Ben into more trouble than he bargained for. He was arrested and imprisoned most everywhere he traveled. He was even sentenced to be hanged at one place. He was never really told why.

Ben was finally freed and promptly sent home. He was put on a ship at Tampico, which was bound for the United States. The Mexican leader warned him to never return.

Colonel Ben Milam was broke and disgusted. He never received a deed to the land he had been promised in Texas. Nor was there any mention of the silver mines. He had spent all the money he had earned as a trader with the Comanches. And he was not paid one *peso* for his hard years of service to the country.

Chapter 7

No Rewards

Colonel Benjamin Rush Milam paced up and down the deck of the ship that was bound for his homeland. When the grim-faced passenger stopped to gaze toward the shore, he spotted Mexico off in the distance. He clenched his fists. He set his jaw, and his mouth went hard. Anger swept through his tall, tired body.

He was thinking of how he had helped to strike that country's last blow for their freedom. He had entered in an agreement that was fair and square. He had expected a fair shake. But Ben had been double-crossed, and everything had turned sour.

You're a foreigner! You're a foreigner! You're a foreigner! The words kept ringing in his ears.

Ben's dreams were smashed like the angry waves

upon a rocky coast. He had been so happy about settling in Texas. He wanted to see its forests again, along with the herds of wild horses running through the grassy meadows. He wondered if they would ever let him settle in that great country, which was no longer claimed by Spain. It belonged to Mexico now.

By rights, he should have been in Texas looking for a place to settle down. And he would have had enough money to get started if Mexico had paid him off. And those silver mines, those visions of treasures and hidden riches, vanished along with his dreams.

Some of the anger finally began to leave Ben. The waves were working their magic upon the battle-worn hero of the Spanish-Mexican Revolution. He had meant well in trying to help set up a government for the people. He guessed they just didn't understand each other.

His spirit was badly bent, but they had not broken it. However, he had no idea of what he would do in the future. All he knew was that he was still alive.

James Long had not been so lucky. He had died. The thoughts of that fatal day still pricked Ben like a mesquite thorn. He knew that his first task was to locate Long's wife, Jane, and give her the things that belonged to her late husband.

When he finally found her, Ben saw her through the tough time. He helped her move and helped her build a new log cabin. Ben even hand-cut the boards and wooden pegs. Needless to say, Jane was very grateful.

Ben was happy to help a friend. But as time went on, he began to notice her smile a little more and the spirited way she walked. He caught himself watching her every move. He had never felt like that about a woman before.

It was time for him to move on, but he didn't want to leave. He was in love with Jane Long. So he told her he loved her. And he asked the beautiful woman if she would be his wife.

Color rose in the widow's cheeks. She was not ready for this. There were too many memories of her James. It seemed as if she would never answer.

"I could never give my heart and hand but to one man," she finally said.

It took Ben a little while to come to his senses. But he tried to understand. He untied his horse, swung up to the saddle, and rode away to find a place of his own.

In the meantime, reports had reached Ben that new leaders had come to power in Mexico. New leaders meant new plans. Ben thought he might get what was coming to him after all.

He headed out for Kentucky to get his baptismal

certificate proving he was a Catholic. Catholicism was the required religion of Mexico. He would get his old buddies to write letters saying he was of good character and sound mind. Off he went, back to his old Kentucky homeplace.

Springtime was a great time to return. The bluegrass was in bloom, and tiny blossoms carpeted the pastures like a thick blue rug. It was planting time, and fields had been readied for a new crop. Ben noticed the snails crawling upon the weeds in the flowery meadows. Old-timers said that meant rain. And a good shower would make the seeds sprout. Before long, little plants would be popping up through the rich loamy soil.

Ben got the royal treatment when he arrived. His family was so happy to have him back. The dogs barked their greetings, wagged their tails of welcome, and gave him lots of warm, slurpy licks.

His kinfolks and friends gathered around. Everyone asked him questions about his daring adventures. It was an exciting time.

Later, Ben broke the news that he was returning to Mexico. He told them that he had to find out if he had a chance of regaining his fortune.

His brothers discouraged him. They feared he would be risking his life if he went back. More than likely, he would end up with more broken promises—if he survived. His father said his other sons had found plenty of land to plow in Kentucky and Ben could too, if he had the mind to.

But his mother looked into the serious, dark eyes of her handsome son. She seemed to understand. This was something Ben had to do. His mind was set. She agreed it was time for him to strike out against an injustice.

Milams had always stood up for what they believed in. She reminded her husband that they had been among the first pioneers to go over the Blue Ridge Mountains and the bluegrass region. They came to make a new home. Their folks did not want them to go. They were warned about the dangers of that wild Kentucky territory. Before that, Ben's Welsh grandfather had not paid any heed to warnings, cither. He braved the stormy seas to settle in America. He, too, did what he had to do.

It was then that she gave Ben his madstone. The magic rock was always presented to a member of the family when starting a new home. She felt sure her son would win his case and soon settle down.

She put the chunky stone into Ben's outstretched hand. It was about the size of an apple, but it was a little flat on one side. It had tiny holes much like the pores of the skin. This one had been found in the stomach of a deer.

Ben was very thankful, especially after she told him she had saved this extra-special white one just for him. He stashed it away for safekeeping. He surely did not want to lose it.

In those days, people used the madstone for all kinds of bites. They believed it was as good for drawing out rattlesnake venom as it was for bites from rabid animals, such as cats, dogs, and skunks.

Ben's mother gave him the general directions for using the madstone: "Soak the stone in hot milk and apply on the bite. The stone will fall off when it has soaked up as much poison as it can hold. Drop the stone in hot milk and swish it around until clean. Repeat this until the stone will no longer stay on. Always keep a fresh pot of hot milk ready for the next cleaning. Do this until the treatment is over."

(Today no one uses the madstone. We have doctors to help us get well.)

Ben left with the letters and the certificate—and his madstone. On his return mission to Mexico he knew the first thing he had to do was visit General Trespalacios, who now lived in northern Mexico. He hoped to get a good reference from this man. And he might have a chance to get what was coming to him.

Chapter 8

The Big Chance

Strange as it may seem, Trespalacios did come to Ben Milam's aid. He went into great detail on behalf of his young colonel. He wrote it was only right that they give Milam what was due him. A list was included.

Ben was grateful. But the prospects were still slim. He had to get the final okay at Mexico City, and that was so far away. He knew very well that he was taking a risk by traveling alone. And he still shuddered when he thought of how he had been run out of the country. The warning never to return whizzed through his mind like a tail-twisting tornado.

But he had to go on. This might be his only chance. He must make his re-entry into the nation's capital very carefully.

Mexico was still an unhappy country. He had no way of knowing how things would go for him.

Luckily, Ben arrived safely. He took his stand before the officials and presented his letters and the certificate.

Ben told the new leaders of the republic that he believed in what they stood for. He said that he wanted to join the army and become a Mexican citizen. He vowed to obey the laws of the land. He would fight side by side with their soldiers to gain the democracy and peace they were working toward.

They listened to his plea and read his papers, but they stopped when they came to the request for land. One of the officers glanced up and asked why he wanted this. Ben's face reddened at the question. His first impulse was to snap back that he had earned it. But he simmered down and gained control of himself.

Ben replied, truthfully, that he wanted to live there because it was such a fine country. He explained that he had been in and out of the territory many times. And something always pulled him back. He wanted to settle down, and knew he could make it. His pioneer father had taught him about settling in a new country. And he could help others who wanted to make a new home in this great land west of the Mississippi River.

No questions ever came up about his other requests. Ben had no idea how the men felt about any of that.

He waited for days and days. The only reply he was able to get out of them was *"mañana."* He knew all too well that the word meant "tomorrow." It could also mean that they might put him off until the next day—or forever.

Ben thought about heading back, but he couldn't do it. He would just try to stay calm and keep out of trouble the best he could.

Finally, he was summoned to appear before the court. He guessed the time had come for a showdown.

The judge told Ben they had observed his actions during his long stay there. They liked what they saw. They were convinced that he would be a good citizen of Mexico.

And so, Benjamin Rush Milam became a Mexican citizen. Never again could he be called a foreigner. This meant that he had all the same rights and privileges as any other law-abiding citizen of that country.

Ben was inducted into the Mexican army and was commanded to stay on as colonel. This appointment came as a complete surprise. There had been no mention of it before.

Ben got his land—lots of land. It was more than

he could have gained in a whole lifetime back in Kentucky. He was given permission to choose where he wanted to settle.

He knew exactly where he wanted to live. It was in the Red River Valley at the northeastern corner of Texas. He had found the spot when he trekked up the river one time from New Orleans. He never really expected such a thing to come about. But now it had.

Oddly enough, this country was very much like his home. There was good grass for raising cattle, fertile soil to grow crops, and plenty of trees to build a cabin and corncribs.

Ben also would become the owner of some silver mines, either by purchase or as a gift. They were known to be some of the richest in Mexico.

Thoughts of those dreary days in jail cells seemed to fade away. A feeling of happiness surged through his well-worn body. He had never felt like this before.

Plans were popping up in Ben Milam's head at ninety miles a minute as he jogged the long way home. He was going to be busier than a squirrel storing away hickory nuts for its winter rations. He would send for Jefferson Milam, his nephew, to come to his aid. Jeff was a surveyor and could help him measure off the land.

He knew he would have to start from scratch. It

would take a lot of hard work. But he and Jeff could handle it.

And those silver mines? They were scattered here, there, and everywhere. He decided he would go about the business of staking out those claims later on. *Mañana?* No, maybe sooner than that.

Chapter 9

Ups and Downs

When Ben Milam reached the Red River Valley, he grabbed a clod of the red clay dirt and crumbled it in his fist. This was his. He had acres and acres of these rich bottom lands—farther than his eyes could see.

He bought himself some cattle and laid in a supply of goods. He was champing at the bits to tame those wild horses grazing in the valley. Things were moving along so well, he even took a job as an agent to help a friend settle some lands.

But there were setbacks. When the land was surveyed, they found out that it was in the state of Arkansas. Ben had moved over too far to the east. The governor of that state would not honor his Mexican title.

There was a big fuss about these border lands. And it looked like this would be going on for some time. Odds were that Ben would lose his spread. And it chilled him to see settlers from the United States staking claims in his so-called territory.

But Ben was never one to give up. There was plenty of land on the frontier. He squared his broad shoulders and moved on down deeper into Texas.

January 12, 1826, was a great day in the life of Ben Milam. The determined adventurer succeeded in getting a grant of land on that day. This contract was somewhat different from the first one. He became an *empresario* like his neighbor, Stephen F. Austin. This meant that he was the leader of a whole colony. He was to bring in three hundred families by a certain time. Then he would receive a bounty of land as a reward.

"Milam's Colony" was a strip of land that stretched between the banks of the Colorado and Guadalupe rivers. It bordered the Old San Antonio Road on the east and widened westward toward the upper reaches of the Balcones Escarpment. This very hilly region is now known as the Devil's Backbone. Comanche territory began on the other side of this formation.

This long, narrow colony had many sparkling springs and creeks. The wooded hills and valleys had good mesquite grass for grazing. Ben was no stranger to these parts because of his travels back and forth to Comanche land. He liked what he saw. He grinned as he thought of how lucky he was after all to have a legal, tax-free contract.

Ben heard that another fellow Kentuckian had also put down roots in Texas. The man had settled somewhere up near the Red River. His name was Collin McKinney.

One fine day, in between moves, Ben decided to check this out. Jeff joined him in the search.

One story says that when they topped a hill they spotted a creek. The two decided it would be a good place to water their horses. As they made their way down, they heard voices. But they couldn't make out what was being said for the babbling water.

Then they caught sight of two girls wading in the stream. Girls were fairly rare in those parts, especially pretty ones. So the riders wasted no time in hitching their horses to a tree. They hurried toward the startled girls.

Ben told them he was looking for a man from his own state of Kentucky. His name was McKinney. Ben asked if they could help him. The girls' faces reddened as they faced the strangers. The older one spoke out. Imagine Ben and Jeff's surprise when they heard her say that the man was their father.

Annie and Elizabeth directed the horsebackers to their home. The family gave them a warm welcome. They had a feast of chicken, fresh greens, cornbread, and apple pie for dessert. It wasn't often that they had visitors, especially from the land of the bluegrass.

Ben returned to talk over the problems of the country every chance he had. It helped to discuss things with the older man. Somehow he felt better, even if he didn't always follow the advice given.

He wanted to show his appreciation to his friend in some way. But he didn't have much to give. Ben thought and thought. What could one give a man who had everything?

He thought about his madstone. But how could he ever part with that? He had carried it with him for so long. It is not known whether Ben ever used it or not. But like his gun, it was precious to him.

He reasoned that he could not divide his gun. But folks had been known to divide the madstone. This one was big enough to divide into two good-sized pieces. And the break would not affect the magic powers of either piece. So that's just what he did for his trusted friend.

McKinney was deeply touched by the gift. The old patriot told Ben that he would keep the madstone for the rest of his life. Then someday it would be passed on to his children. And it was.

The father was not the only friend that Ben had in this household. The son, William, liked him, too.

The boy looked forward to the times when Ben loped in for another visit. He never tired of hearing about the scary adventures of the handsome warrior. And the girls? Business and storytelling weren't the only reasons Ben and Jeff Milam paid a call to the McKinneys from time to time. Jeff had taken a liking to Elizabeth. And Ben admired Annie.

Annie had been on Ben's mind ever since he first saw her. When she smiled or gave the faintest wink, it melted him down like butter.

Ben fell in love with her. He wanted to ask her to marry him. But it wasn't easy. He got tongue-tied. Whatever he had to say never seemed to come out right.

Finally, he worked up enough nerve to pop the question. It took a while for Ben to grasp her answer. He just couldn't believe she had really said yes. Happiness washed over him like a spring shower.

The blushing bride-to-be started making plans for their wedding. But just before they were completed, Ben got some bad news from Mexico. It was about the silver mines. His business associate in land and mining deals sent word that they were having problems. Ben needed to come as soon as possible.

Ben told Annie that he must go and straighten things out before they tied the knot. He promised to return as soon as possible. Needless to say, it was a tearful farewell.

The silver project was in trouble. Ben's contract read that all the mines had to be worked at the owner's expense. If he did not keep them open, the Mexican government would take them back.

Ben and his partner could not keep *one* mine going at this time, much less twenty-two. The only way they could do so was to borrow the money. He could sell out, form a company, or sell shares of stock. But who had that kind of money? Maybe some of his Kentucky friends would be interested. Or perhaps his old friend, David Burnet, would want to join in a venture.

Ben rode miles and miles on horseback to check up on the mines in the mountains of Mexico. Some of them had already been closed. They had been worked out, and the miners had deserted the camps.

Troubles were piling up quickly, and Ben had to do something about it.

Chapter 10

Rewards and Losses

In the spring of 1828, Ben Milam reached Mexico City again. The nation's capital was in a beautiful valley shaped like a big bowl. It was surrounded by snow-capped mountains that were once fiery volcanoes. Tree-lined streets were bordered by bright flowers of many colors. The great plaza, called the *zócalo*, was in the heart of the city.

Fronting the plaza was the National Palace of the president. Ben remembered it for good and bad reasons. When he was a member of the freedom troops, he was housed on a lower floor there.

On this day soldiers still stood guard, but it was more peaceful than it was back in those days. Lovers promenaded, and people were going about the business of carrying on the government.

People still remembered him. He felt honored that they still hailed him as one of the liberators of freedom.

But Ben was anxious to get the silver problems solved as quickly as possible. He found that his partner had formed the English Mining Company without telling Ben about the deal. The Englishmen had broken their contract and refused to send the money that was due.

Ben was told that the deal was not worth a hill of *frijoles* (beans). Mexico could not force payment. These people were liable for their debts under their own laws. The only thing left to do was either forget about the whole thing, or go to England and press charges.

It was a long, long way over to that country, farther even than South America. Ben cringed at the thought of going.

But old rough-and-ready wasn't going to tackle the problem sitting down. He knew he must meet it head on. Away he sailed to England.

Ben and his advisers were in and out of the British courts, pleading their case for many months. Then, once and for all, he won on the last appeal that could be made. Both sides agreed upon a settlement. It was not a deal that would make him wealthy, but it was far better than nothing. Ben's part was said to be a little more than $2,500.

While he was there, Ben tried to get the English folks to buy into his colony. But he had no luck at all with the idea. The money lenders said it was too risky. They were not willing to put up any cash until the country was better settled and titles were guaranteed.

The first thing Ben thought of after those deals was to buy Annie something—something extra special. After shopping around, he decided on some silverware and a mahogany table. This was a very elegant piece of furniture, crafted by skilled artisans. Few plantation owners could afford the likes of such a table for their Sunday-best parlors.

He wondered what Annie was doing. It had been so long since he last saw her. He should have written, but he couldn't spell well at all. He had to have help in writing his legal papers. But he'd go to blazes before he let anyone in on his love affair.

Ben made it back to the McKinneys as soon as he could after his return to Texas. He could just imagine Annie's face lighting up as he presented her with the bridal gifts.

But Ben knew the minute he laid eyes on Annie that something was wrong. She looked so startled. There was no smile on her pretty face, and no twinkle in her eyes. She just stood there like a wooden doll.

Then, in a slow, unsteady voice, she told him

that since she had not heard from him for almost three years, she had given him up as missing. She had found someone else.

Chapter 11

New Threats

Ben had despair written all over his downcast face. His dreams were toppling like the falling leaves of autumn.

The grueling trip had been made for nothing. He felt betrayed and angry. But he could not go on moping the rest of his life about a lost love.

It took all the grit he could muster to tell Annie that he was a forgiving man. He wished her the best and told her goodbye.

There was a heap of things piled up for Ben to do. But first, he decided to take the silver and table to Elizabeth. He knew that she and Jeff could use them.

In his own words he said, "Eliza, I am going to

give you these things I brought for Annie. I haven't time for women anyway. My country needs me."

Ben wasted no time in galloping off to see his lawyer friend, David Burnet. The two had talked about silver some years back when they were visiting their Comanche friends. Maybe David would know how to make some of the mines pay off.

They drew up a plan and decided to start the Western Mining and Colonization Company. They would sell shares of stock, much like was done in the deal between England and Mexico. Then they would use the money to put the mines into production. Both agreed to split the profit.

But before long, they ran into trouble. The salesman who sold the shares failed to explain the terms of the contract correctly. The stockholders became confused and unhappy. There were even threats to sue the company.

Ben and David were honest men trying to get a good business going. They were shocked when they heard all this bad news. The two worked very hard to clear up the misunderstanding. But the damage had been done. The company was going down, and the partners decided to call the whole thing off.

Again, the mines were put on hold. The rich veins of silver ore would stay hidden beneath the ground for the time being.

It was high time Ben got his act together and settled his colony. Time was running out, and he would have to work every day and far into the night to fulfill the contract of settling his colony.

It would not be easy. His grant was not as easy to get to as some of the other areas in Texas. It was hard to maneuver covered wagons up and down those steep hills. Some folks turned away and went trudging on to other places.

Also, the Comanches had started raiding the settlers because they were invading their territory. They distrusted the white men.

People had heard stories that grew wilder with each telling about this Comanche territory. The newcomers could just imagine thousands of red men swooping down, raiding and killing and robbing.

But something else worried Ben more than a few skirmishes with men who wore feathers in their hair. It was the Mexicans. They were part of the reason those Comanches were going on rampages in the first place.

He knew very well where the Indians' ammunition was coming from. It was the same kind he had used when he helped the Mexicans win their freedom. His adopted country had promised the colonists protection. So why were they supporting the Indian raids?

This was a traumatic discovery for Ben. It was like an oncoming tornado threatening to destroy the land and its people. Ben didn't have to be able to read or write like a New York lawyer to know that this spelled trouble. And trouble it was!

Chapter 12

The Breaking Point

The Mexican Law of April 6, 1830, came like a bolt of lightning out of the sky. The edict stated there would be no more *norteamericanos* (North Americans) in Texas. Only Mexicans and people from other countries besides the United States would be allowed to enter. And settlers would have to pay taxes on all foreign goods. Troops would be sent to see that the law was carried out.

This was a decree of broken promises. People were losing their freedom. The action would lead Texas toward a revolution.

Many North Americans were turned back at the borders. Some slipped through. Others did not bother to try. Ben's colony was one of the hardest hit. He had not reached his quota of settlers, which meant that he would probably be unable to complete his contract.

The Texans had to find another way to get their goods out and to buy things without having to pay such high taxes. Mexican troops were already arriving to collect fees on goods coming in and to check on goods that settlers were shipping out.

There had to be a way to bypass these troops. Some settlers thought they could send their goods down the Red River to New Orleans. But the problem was that big boats could not go very far upstream. Logs, mud, and trash had been piling up for years, clogging the stream. And no one had done anything about it. It would be impossible to clear such a sluggish stream, they said.

But they really didn't know Ben Milam. He would tackle anything, no matter how tough it was. Ben decided to give it a try.

The great-hearted daredevil lost no time. He bought a steamboat at his own expense and steered toward the mass on the upper waters. Tying ropes onto the jammed trees, he pulled them over to the riverbanks with his boat. Then he dived into the murky waters and hooked onto the sunken logs. Men with mule teams were waiting to drag them away.

Ben ran the risk of sinking his boat and maybe even losing his life. But on he chopped and tugged and pulled. After a time he cleared the channel. Ben Milam was the first person to get a steamboat up that part of the Red River. It was ready for traffic—for a while, at least.

Steamboats loaded with cotton, hides, and produce were chugging down to the new markets. This gave the people some hope, especially to those in the Red River Valley. And Ben was their hero.

But there were other pressing problems, even though Mexico had eased up on the new law. Many settlers did not have titles to their property. Greedy land speculators were casting a wary eye toward those who had no papers to show ownership. They were threatening to kick these people out of their homes and leave them to roam in the wilderness.

None of the people in Ben's colony had received their titles. He had about fifty settlers, which was a far cry from the 300 he was supposed to have. And to his sorrow, his contract had expired.

Ben wanted to help these people get their legal claims, even though his contract was no longer good. For some reason, he still managed to hold part of the land that was due him.

Life was getting harder and harder in Texas. Gaps were growing wider and wider. No one knew what or whom to believe.

Again, all eyes shifted toward Ben Milam. The people looked to him for help. He had been in fights with Mexico and had managed to come out shining like a bright new *peso*. They persuaded him to return to Mexico and plead for their rights. He left some of his personal belongings with McKinney and made ready for the trip to the capital. It would be to Monclova, for this was the capital of the province that Texas had been linked to.

Monclova was in an uproar, too. The people were divided on political issues. General Antonio López de Santa Anna had been elected president. And he soon became a dictator. He threw the laws of the constitution out the window. He was forgetting the rights of the people. His spies were known to be working in the city.

Ben tried to stay cool, calm, and collected. But he was suspicious of all that was going on. He sensed he was being watched, as a mouse is watched by a cat. Despite the eerie feeling, he was able to clear up the title troubles. He and some of his friends quickly took to the byways to get out of there.

Yet the champion of human rights got into more trouble than he bargained for. The group was waylaid by Santa Anna's troops and taken off to prison. They were separated from each other.

When that iron door slammed shut, Ben Milam knew he was in deep trouble. He looked about the darkened cell with dismay. The smell turned his stomach. His face went white. Horror was in his eyes.

A Mexican colonel arrested as a suspicious foreigner? No, it couldn't be. He had risked his life to save these people. It was not fair to be treated like an illegal alien. He wouldn't believe anything they said anymore.

He swore in the darkness against Mexico and Santa Anna and that brother-in-law of his by the name of Martín Perfecto de Cós. He was bitter at the whole world.

If he ever got out of here, he would never come back—not for all the land titles in the world.

Mexican soldiers were marching past the prison walls. Wheels went rumbling by all day and far into the night. News was passed that they were on their way to wipe out the Texans. Those were fighting words!

Texans needed Ben Milam like they never needed him before. But he was trapped. Nothing could save him now. He had no chance to escape. His hope was ebbing away, little by little, day by day.

Ben was moved from prison to prison for over four months. Each time he was let out under heavy guard. He knew he would eventually have to face the firing squad. He just didn't know when.

Ben was relieved when he was put in the prison

at Monterrey. To his surprise, he had some freedom. He could even take a bath in the nearby stream.

He found that he knew some of his fellow prisoners. And he was treated kindly by the law officers. Had they heard of his services to their country and felt he had been given a raw deal? Ben had come to the conclusion that it wasn't the people, but the *leader*, that he was against.

A pretty *señorita*, who was the daughter of the jailer, came to his cell one afternoon. The girl smiled as she handed him a key through the bars. She pointed toward the bath place.

It took a wild moment to understand what was going on. Suddenly, her actions started to make sense to him. At sundown, Milam escaped past the sentinel.

He made tracks to the place he was to go. Moments later, he spotted a horse that was saddled and ready to ride. Saddlebags were bulging.

What luck! He mounted up and took off as fast as his horse would take him.

Chapter 13

Decision at Goliad

The moon was showing upon the horizon. The North Star was lighted like a candle to guide Benjamin Rush Milam on his flight to freedom. He had followed that star, thanks to his father, all these years. It had never failed to lead him in the right direction.

At daylight, Ben sacked out under the trees. He had decided it was safer to ride by night and lay up in the shade during the day. There were enough rations in the saddlebags to keep him alive for a while. He ate sparingly to make them last as long as possible. And he was able to find a few watercourses amid stands of trees along the way.

But soon the trees played out. Ben had no cover for protection. He was dying of thirst. The food was about gone. He had been riding so long that he was saddle sore. He must have traveled for miles and miles.

If his memory served him right, he should have been at the Rio Grande by now. But he wasn't. There were no signs that he was even near the stream.

He grew wearier by the day. His sleepy eyes scanned the sky for his star to point the way. And he rode on.

At last, he reached the "Big River," the Rio Grande. Both man and beast got their fill of water. Ben thought he could make it the rest of the way, traveling during the day.

One afternoon Ben stopped off by a clump of mesquite trees. He was too tired to drag on any further. He collapsed under the thorny branches and went to sleep.

Sometime later he was awakened by the sound of horses clomping their hooves. Had the enemy been tracking him? Did they know all this time where he was?

They were coming closer. Voices were getting louder. They were upon him. All was lost.

A horse skidded in fright at the sight of the crumpled escapee. The rider reined his steed, then yelled to find who was there.

Ben straightened up. That was the most welcome shout he had ever heard. The man had spoken in English! There was a lot of talk out in the middle of nowhere, near the town of Goliad.

The small group of volunteers briefed Ben on what had been going on while he was gone. Winds of revolution had spread throughout the settlements like a Texas brushfire.

They said that Texans had no choice but to defend their rights. The revolution had not been officially declared, but many were already in the fight. Gonzales had just won their battle over a cannon.

This group was on their way to nearby Presidio La Bahía at Goliad to rout a Mexican military unit. Mexican General Cós had left a task force there as he made his way toward San Antonio.

They pleaded with Ben to join them in driving out those soldiers before they had time to strike out at the settlers.

None of those volunteers could possibly feel the pain Ben was going through at this moment. It took him back to the time he had answered Mexico's call for help in their struggle for their rights. Mexico was his country. And he remembered how he had sworn on a Bible to be true to its government.

He would be giving up his Mexican citizenship. Chances were he would lose everything that he had. He might never be a landowner again, and probably wouldn't have another opportunity to rework his mines. This would be slamming the door shut on all his dreams.

Ben knew there were many good Mexican people, and he would never forget the ones who had helped him settle his land and silver problems. Those poor people in that village who had saved his life—the ones he had hoped to repay with a spinning wheel someday—and the girl who had helped to free him from prison ... There were many more he was grateful to.

But that was more than he could say about some of the others he had met. He had been kicked and stomped and thrown in every jail between there and Mexico City. They never trusted him. He was just another paleface from across the Rio Grande to be watched and spied on.

General Santa Anna was out to destroy Texas, which was Ben's real homeland. His blood started to boil at the thought of living under the rules of a dictator. Yes, he must get into the fight.

The determined veteran of revolutions fell in line with his comrades. There were forty-eight volunteers. They divided into four groups, one of which was to watch the horses. Ben Milam was the leader of one of the groups that would invade the place.

The Presidio La Bahía straddled a chalky, flat-topped hill that overlooked the San Antonio River valley. The stone fort was built by the Spaniards many years earlier. That night, under the moonlight, the famous landmark cast ghostly shadows over the Texans as they made their attack.

Quickly, the little band stormed the fort. The sentry was knocked out cold. They chopped down a door and then blasted into the sleeping quarters before the Mexicans knew what was going on.

The startled captives surrendered. And on the night of October 9, 1835, the volunteers captured the Presidio La Bahía. They were now in possession of a lot of valuable loot—cannon, guns, ammunition, and a heap of other supplies. It was enough to outfit an army. But most important, they had cut off the Mexican army's main supply line to their troops near San Antonio.

Benjamin Rush Milam turned to his winning countrymen and said, "The events of this night have fully compensated me for all my losses and all my sufferings."

Chapter 14

"Who Will Go?"

It was Ben Milam's duty to take the prisoner officers to General Stephen F. Austin. The general and
his small army were stationed out from Gonzales.
Austin, too, had just returned from Mexico after a
long term of imprisonment.

Austin and his army were headed toward San
Antonio in hopes of making an attack upon General
Cós. And they needed to know what was going on
along the way.

Ben volunteered to be in charge of a company of
scouts sent to spy upon the Mexicans. He was told
to select the safest route for the army to follow,
capture any guard that might be blocking passage
along the San Antonio River, keep undercover, and
avoid suspicion of the enemy at all times. Also, after

this mission, he might have to venture to the Rio Grande to see what was going on there.

This was a challenge to Ben Milam. It made sense to invade San Antonio. The city was the main hub of activity for both Texas and Mexico. If they could take it, Texans could then be in control of the whole territory. He was ready to go at the drop of his cap.

The trail-smart leader and his men made their way toward the city. He knew the lay of the land like the back of his hand.

They stalked the enemy for weeks, and sent back messages to their advancing commander-in-chief, Stephen Austin. These men were like shadows lurking through the trees and bushes. They knew that to kick a rock or break a tree limb could cause an alert. The Mexicans also had scouts in the woods, and odds were in their favor.

Meanwhile, back in the army camp, they were having problems. The men were restless and grouchy. They griped about having to sleep out in the rain. Some said they hadn't had a good meal in weeks. They were running out of food supplies.

To make matters worse, the members of the Consultation, who were now meeting at San Felipe, appointed General Stephen F. Austin as a commissioner to go to the United States. He was ordered to leave at once and find men, money, and supplies for the army.

Colonel Edward Burleson was elected the new commander-in-chief to take General Austin's place. He immediately called a council of war. The main issue at stake was whether to attack now or later. They argued about when the invasion should take place.

They finally decided it would be a disaster to go against such a mighty army during the winter season. They would wait until spring. But some disagreed with this decision. They feared what could happen to their army in the future if it disbanded.

When Ben Milam returned from his scouting mission, he could not believe what he saw. Supply wagons were loaded, bags were packed, and horses were already saddled for the march.

The battered veteran did not understand such a decision. He had never walked away from a fight.

Reinforcements had just arrived from the United States. Word had spread that Texas was in deep trouble. Men had come from all over the country with loaded guns. They were ready to fight. The quicker the better.

The men had turned a deaf ear when a Mexican defector said that all was not well in the Cós camp. And some hardly listened to their own spy, who had just returned with news that the enemy's stronghold was weakening.

There was a faint glimmer of hope in Ben Milam's mind after he heard the report from the spy. It meant that Cós was open to an attack. Now was the time to strike for freedom—not next spring. They must storm the city that very night in a surprise attack.

Ben shook his head as he looked out over the scattering crowd. He was afraid that once these men split up and spread out over the countryside, all hope would be lost. Texas was a great country, and it was worth fighting for.

The brave leader of men could not stand there any longer with his arms folded. It was time to get into action. He must get the men to stay.

Ben felt he was a better soldier than he was a speaker. He had depended upon his lawyer friends to do that for him. But since none of them were around, he had to speak for himself—but fast.

The fighter for justice got the nod from his commander-in-chief and climbed upon a wagon. His flashing, dark eyes showed no sign of fear. He yelled out to get the attention of the milling crowd. His stern, booming voice echoed throughout the valley. The frontiersmen turned their heads toward the lone figure who held his rifle high over his head.

Boldly, he made his plea, "WHO WILL GO WITH OLD BEN MILAM INTO SAN ANTONIO?"

That set the crowd off. Men threw their hats and coonskin caps into the air. And they shouted to the top of their voices that they were ready to march. Ben got their message.

He shouted back, "Then fall in line!"

Over three hundred answered the command. These were brave men who believed in the cause. They just needed someone like Ben Milam to fire them up.

Colonel Benjamin Rush Milam called his first meeting. They gathered under the trees near an old mill on the banks of the San Antonio River.

The troops were grouped into two divisions. Colonel Milam was to lead the first group. Colonel Frank W. Johnson would lead the other. General Burleson would hold some reserves in readiness at the river camp.

The De la Garza and Veramendi houses were chosen as headquarters. The old homes had thick walls and were close enough together for the leaders to exchange messages. They were also within range of the enemy riflemen.

These patriots did not look like an army. They had no uniforms. They were not even legal soldiers, for Texas had not officially declared war against Mexico.

But they were now one and the same in spirit. They were as tough as rawhide.

Off they marched toward San Antonio in the dark of the night. They were going to take on an army more than four times their size.

Chapter 15

The Last Stand

San Antonio was clustered around a group of missions, the most famous of which was the Alamo. Many rich and well-known people lived there. The old river city was usually a quiet and orderly place, very much like during the days of the Spaniards.

But not this evening. The main plaza was crowded with soldiers of the Mexican army. They were having a good time in the town. Musicians were playing. Some were dancing with graceful *señoritas*. Many were tipping the jug. *Tortillas* were going as fast as the cooks could flip them off the iron plates.

Still, there was a sense of danger in the air. General Cós had placed cannons at strategic points of the city. The cobblestone streets were barricaded. Barracks were fortified.

The Mexican battle flag was flapping in the wind atop the arches of the Alamo nearby. The old fortress was to be used mainly as a place for light artillery. All of this preparation was made in case unruly bands of Texans attempted to enter the city.

What they did not know, amid all this merry-making, was that those wily Texans were advancing toward the city at that moment. They would soon be pitching camp and making ready for the big shootout. All was going as planned.

But just as the Texas army was entering their headquarters, a Mexican guard fired at them. One of Ben's men made the tragic mistake of firing back. This was a dead giveaway to the enemy that they were under attack.

The Mexican army immediately started a heavy bombardment. There was a thunderous roll of cannon fire and the crack of rifles. Protective walls were leveled, and houses were battered.

The only thing the tired and worn Texas force could do was to fortify their quarters. They knocked out holes in the walls and windows to shoot from. Others made sandbags to pile around the walls and doors. It was a risky job getting the sand scooped up and getting back to safety.

They fired only when they spotted an enemy

looking over the walls or caught sight of one in an opening. This went on all day and far into the night.

Some of Burleson's reserves had been able to smuggle in enough beef to fill their empty stomachs. The food helped to keep up their morale.

By the second day, the Texans were ready to get with it. Colonel Milam, with Colonel Johnson's help, had planned their strategy. Every soldier knew what they had to do.

The bottom line was, "Get 'em boys! Go house to house, room to room, until you get 'em all cleaned out!"

The fighting was brutal. Artillery fire was hot and heavy. Bullets were whizzing from all over. But Colonel Ben Milam kept on fighting beside his men all the way.

By the middle of the day they had fought the Mexicans to a draw. Slowly they were making headway. By nightfall, enemy bombardment had slackened up a bit. Colonel Milam felt that his plan was working. The Mexicans had not been trained to combat this guerrilla way of fighting.

The third day was not quite so fierce. But the fight was still on. The Texans kept smashing doors and taking over.

By midafternoon the Mexican forces began to weaken faster. Their soldiers, many of whom were ex-convicts, were running to the rear to get away from the straight-shooting Texans.

Colonel Milam knew he had the enemy where he wanted them. The battle would soon be won.

He stepped into the courtyard on his way to contact Colonel Johnson about winding down the battle. But he never made it. He was mortally wounded by a sniper in a nearby cypress tree. Ben Milam had fought his last battle on that wintry afternoon of December 7, 1835.

Emotions were strong among the men for their brave and loyal colonel. They fought on like wildcats. Two days later, General Cós raised the white flag of defeat. He promised to leave Texas.

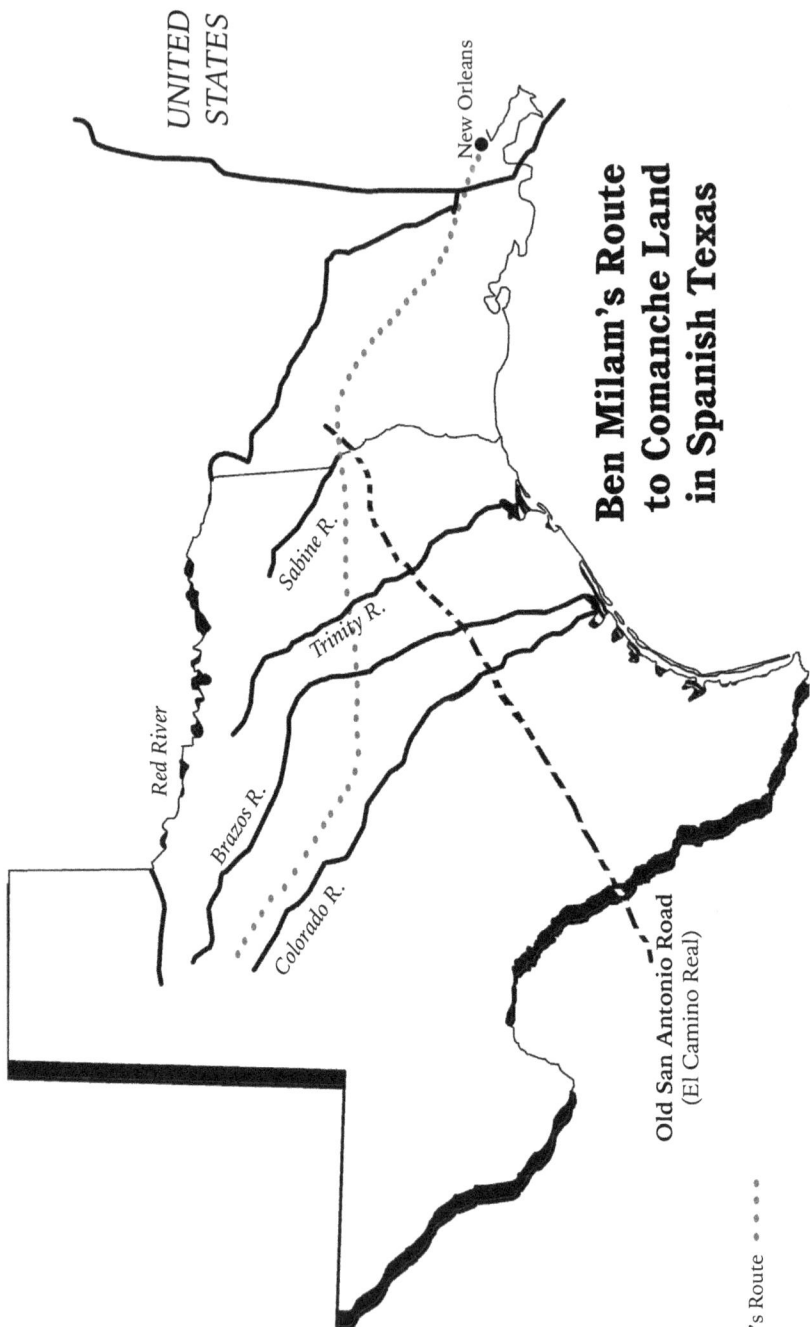

Ben Milam's Route
to Comanche Land
in Spanish Texas

UNITED STATES

New Orleans

Red River

Sabine R.

Trinity R.

Brazos R.

Colorado R.

Old San Antonio Road
(El Camino Real)

Ben Milam's Route • • • •

Epilogue

A monument now marks Colonel Milam's resting place, which is near the Alamo. Other monuments, like the one in Milam County, have been erected in honor of this fearless leader. Many markers have been placed across the state for the tall Texan.

But perhaps Erastus "Deaf" Smith, one of Colonel Milam's soldiers, said it best at the end of a poem he wrote—"And generations yet unborn shall honor Milam's name."

That famous yell, "Who will go with Old Ben Milam?" continued to urge the settlers to carry on during the dark days that were to come in the Texas Revolution.

Remember Colonel
Benjamin Rush Milam!

Ben Milam's Grant

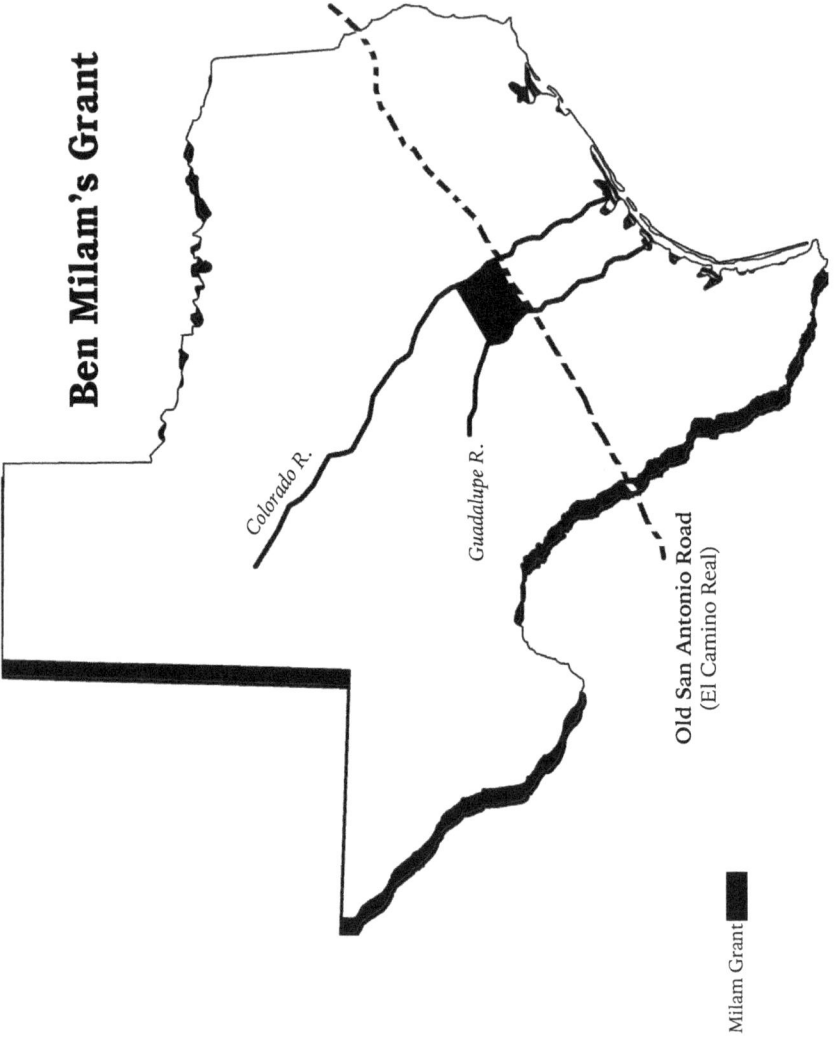

Colorado R.

Guadalupe R.

Old San Antonio Road
(El Camino Real)

Milam Grant

Glossary

artillery: large weapons like cannons
barge: flat-bottomed boat
battered: worn out or damaged
bluegrass: a grass with bluish-green stems
bunch grass: grass that grows in clumps
cornpone: bread made of corn
duds: clothes
empresario: (em preh SAH ree o) Spanish for leader of a colony
frijoles: (free HO les) Spanish for beans
grit: strong spirit
guerrilla: a small band of fighters
hemp: fiber from a tall plant used in making rope
homespuns: made of plain wool
Kentucky Derby: a famous horse race
madstone: a special rock used by settlers who thought it would draw out poisons in a wound
mañana: (muhn YAH nuh) Spanish for tomorrow
peddler: someone who travels to sell products
peso: (PAY so) Mexican currency

The Veramendi palace, San Antonio. A long, low adobe building with iron grills covering the windows. Carved doors are the carriage entrance.
—Courtesy Western History Collections, University of Oklahoma Library

The Alamo as it appeared in the 1880s.
—Courtesy Western History Collections, University of Oklahoma Library

potluck stews: mixture of whatever food that happens to be handy to cook

powwow: an Indian council or meeting

presidio: (pre SID ee oh) fort

promenaded: walked leisurely in public

quota: a designated number assigned to a group

recruits: men who sign up to fight

royalists: loyal soldiers for the king of Spain and not Mexico

schooner: a ship with two or more masts or poles to hold the sail

señorita: (sen yor EE ta) Spanish for an unmarried girl

skirmish: a minor battle

tortilla: (tor TEE ya) flat, thin, and round bread

vittles: what settlers sometimes called food

Viva la independencia: Spanish for "long live independence"

watercourse: a river or brook

wily: full of trickery

yellow fever: disease carried by a mosquito

zócalo: (SO cah lo) public meeting place in a city

The Garrison Chapel at Presidio La Bahia, Goliad, Texas.
—Courtesy Western History Collections, University of Oklahoma Library

Ben Milam monument in Milam Square, San Antonio, 1930.
—Courtesy Western History Collections, University of Oklahoma Library

Bibliography

Books

Boatright, Mody C., Wilson M. Hudson, and Allen Maxwell, eds. *Madstones and Twisters*. Dallas: Southern Methodist University Press, 1958.

Brown, John Henry. *History of Texas From 1685 to 1892*. Vol 1. St. Louis: Becktold and Co., 1892.

O'Connor, Kathryn Stoner. *The Presidio Lu Bahia del Espiritu Santo de Zuniga, 1721 to 1846*. Austin: Von Boeckmann-Jones Co., 1966.

Webb, Walter Prescott, ed. *The Handbook of Texas*. Austin: The Texas State Historical Association, 1952. 3rd vol., 1976.

Newspapers and Magazines

"Belief in the Effeciency of the Madstone." *Frontier Times*. Vol. 1, No. 1, October 1923, p.31.

Crimmins, Colonel M. L. "Ben Milam's Monument." *Frontier Times*, May 1945.

Dobie, J. Frank. "Madstone Yarn Covers East Texas." *American Statesman*, October 16, 1955.

Garver, Lois. "Benjamin Rush Milam." *Southwestern Historical Quarterly*, XXXVIII (1934-1935).

Hall, R. Franklin. "Who Will Go With Old Ben Milam into San Antonio?" *San Antonio Express*, February 2, 1930, Society Section.

Papers of Benjamin Rush Milam. Center for American History, University of Texas at Austin.

For Young Readers Who Want to Know More

Carnes, Ruth Juby. *David Burnet.* Austin: Eakin Press, 1986.

————. *Horseback Government Ad Interim Administration, Republic of Texas 1836.* San Antonio: The Naylor Co., 1974.

Hoff, Carol. *Wilderness Pioneer.* New York: Follett Publishing Co., 1955.

Sinclair, Dorothy Tutt. *Tales of the Texans.* Chapter VIII. Bellaire, TX: Dorothy Sinclair Enterprises, 1985.

Warren, Betsy. *Let's Remember—When Texas Belonged to Mexico.* Dallas: Hendrick-Long Publishing Co., 1982. (Easy Reading.)

————. *Let's Remember—When Texas Belonged to Spain.* Dallas: Hendrick-Long Publishing Co., 1981. (Easy Reading.)

About the Author

Ruth J. Carnes was a teacher for thirty-five years, mostly in Victoria, Texas, before retiring in 1981. Mrs. Carnes received her bachelor's degree from TCU and did graduate studies at the University of Texas and University of Houston. She has held offices in the Texas State Teachers Association, Texas Classroom Teachers Association, Delta Kappa Gamma, and is the author of several other books (including *David Burnet: From New Jersey to Texas*) as well as numerous magazine articles.

www.ingramcontent.com/pod-product-compliance
Lightning Source LLC
Chambersburg PA
CBHW061153040426
42445CB00013B/1669